❦ History *of* Britain ❦

The

Blitz

1939 to 1945

Andrew Langley

Illustrated by John James

Heinemann

HISTORY OF BRITAIN – THE BLITZ
was produced for Heinemann Children's Reference
by Lionheart Books, London

Editor: Lionel Bender
Designer: Ben White
Editorial Assistant: Madeleine Samuel
Picture Researcher: Jennie Karrach
Media Conversion and Typesetting:
 Peter MacDonald

Educational Consultant: Jane Shuter
Editorial Advisors: Andrew Farrow, Paul Shuter

Production Controller: David Lawrence
Editorial Director: David Riley

First published in Great Britain in 1995
by Hamlyn Children's Books,
This edition published in Great Britain in 1996
by Heinemann Children's Reference, an imprint
of Heinemann Educational Publishers, a division of Reed
Educational and Professional Publishing Limited,
Halley Court, Jordan Hill, Oxford OX2 8EJ

MADRID ATHENS PARIS
FLORENCE PRAGUE WARSAW
PORTSMOUTH NH CHICAGO SAO PAULO
SINGAPORE TOKYO MELBOURNE AUCKLAND
IBADAN GABORONE JOHANNESBURG

© Reed Educational and Professional Publishing Ltd 1996

ISBN 0 600 58599 9 Hb   ISBN 0 600 58600 6 Pb

British Library Cataloguing-in-Publication Data.
A catalogue record for this book is available
from the British Library.

Printed in Italy

Acknowledgements
All artwork by John James
Map on page 23 by Hayward Art Group.

Photo credits
Topham Picture Library: pages 7 (centre), 8 (bottom right), 16 (left), 21
(top left, top right, bottom). Hulton Deutsch Collection: pages 4
(left), 6 (bottom left, bottom right), 7 (top), 8 (bottom right), 9, 10 (left,
top, bottom), 12 (top left, top right), 13 (bottom), 15-16, 15 (top left,
centre), 16 (bottom right), 17 (bottom left, bottom right), 19 (centre,
bottom), 20, 22 (bottom left, top right). Imperial War Museum, London:
pages 5 (top), 8 (top left), 11 (centre), 17 (centre). Peter Newark's Military
Pictures: page 5 (bottom left). MARS: page 5 (bottom right). Robert Opie
Collection: pages 6 (top), 10-11, 12 (bottom), 15 (top right: with
Gunnersbury Park Museum, London). Public Record Office: page 18: INF
13/123/6. London Transport Museum: page 19 (top). John Frost
Archives/Daily Mirror: page 22 (bottom right).
Cover: Icons by Jonathan Adams. Cover photos: Bombed house – Magnum
Photos/George Rodger. Bomb poster, Recruiting poster – Peter Newark's
Military Pictures. Picture cards, Policeman and air raid warning – Topham
Picture Source. Underground shelter – Hulton Deutsch.

PLACES TO VISIT

Here are some museums and sites which contain exhibits
about the Blitz. Your local tourist office will be able to tell you
about places to visit in your area. Throughout 1995 there will
be special celebrations and exhibitions to commemorate the
50th anniversary of the end of World War II.

Cabinet War Rooms, London. The underground rooms from
which the Government ran Britain during the War.

Caernarfon Air World, Gwynedd. Includes several World War
II aircraft, with a special Dambusters exhibit.

Coventry Cathedral. A fine new cathedral, completed in
1964 next to the bombed shell of the old one.

Dover Castle and Hellfire Corner, Kent. Beneath the old
castle is a maze of tunnels where the Dunkirk relief was
planned.

Duxford Airfield, Cambridge. The Imperial War Museum's
collection of historic aircraft also includes a reconstruction
of a wartime air raid.

HMS Belfast, London. The largest surviving World War II
battleship, used to support the D-Day landings.

Imperial War Museum, London. Among many special
exhibits are features on the Blitz and the Home Front.

Museum of London. Includes displays and reconstructions of
social life and buildings in wartime London.

Station 146, Norfolk. Preserved wartime control tower once
used by a US Air Force squadron.

Tangmere Military Aviation Museum, Sussex. A famous
Battle of Britain airfield.

Western Approaches, Liverpool. Re-creation of the wartime
bunker where the campaign against German U-boats was
organized.

White Cliffs Experience, Dover. This multi-media show
includes a simulation of an air raid.

Winston Churchill's Britain at War Museum, London.
Includes exhibits about the Home Front, with many sound
effects.

INTRODUCTION

The Second World War, between 1939 and 1945, in Britain is sometimes called 'The People's War'. This is because it didn't just affect the lives of soldiers. Ordinary men, women and children (civilians) were in danger from enemy bombs, rockets and bullets fired by aircraft. Town-dwellers had to spend many nights in air raid shelters or move into the safer countryside.

London and the South-east region of England suffered worst in this 'Blitz', or heavy aerial attack. But German bombers also brought death and damage to cities as far apart as Glasgow, Liverpool, Cardiff, Belfast and Plymouth. Altogether, over 60,000 civilians were killed, and 80,000 badly wounded. Millions more people lost their homes and possessions.

CONTENTS

WAR BEGINS 1939

It was 3 September 1939. Millions of British people, at home or at work, were listening to their radio sets. At 11.15 that morning, they heard the voice of the Prime Minister, Neville Chamberlain. He told them, "This country is at war with Germany."

Germany had been ruled since 1933 by Adolf Hitler and his political party, the Nazis. Hitler wanted to take revenge for Germany's defeat in the First World War of 1914 to 1918. He started in 1938 by taking over Austria. In March 1939, his troops marched into Czechoslovakia. Six months later, they invaded Poland.

Britain and France had promised to help the Poles if they were attacked. The British government now threatened Hitler with war if his troops did not withdraw from Poland by 3 September. Hitler ignored the threat, and the Second World War began. On one side were the Germans and, from 1940, the Italians. The Soviet Union had agreed not to fight them. On the other side were Britain and France.

△ **A newspaper seller displays the dramatic news.** Here is the count-down to war during 1939:
March 15 – Germans invade Czechoslovakia.
August 23 – Germany and the Soviet Union agree not to fight each other.
September 1 – Germans invade Poland.
September 3 – Britain and France declare war on Germany.

▽ **A family listens to the Prime Minister's radio broadcast** about the start of the war. They have already started to prepare for the coming danger. There are blackout curtains over the window to stop room lights showing outside. The girl is about to try on her new gas mask that will protect her from any poison gas in bombs. In case of invasion, British citizens had to carry an identity card like the one on the table.

◁ **British troops retreat from Dunkirk**, France, in late May 1940 as the German forces advanced. The Germans used a new form of attack, called Blitzkrieg (German for 'lightning war'), which was fast and took the enemy by surprise. Large numbers of tanks and soldiers in trucks smashed through Allied defences.

For several months, little happened. The Germans took a strong grip on Poland, and a small British force landed in France. This period was called the Phoney (false) War, since little fighting took place. It ended in April 1940, when German troops invaded Norway then Denmark, Belgium, Luxembourg and the Netherlands. By June, the British army had been driven back across the Channel, and France too had fallen to Hitler's army. Britain and its empire were left alone to face the Nazis. Hitler prepared for 'Operation Sealion' – his invasion of Britain. But first, the Germans had to gain control of the air by defeating the Royal Air Force (RAF). German bombers set out to destroy the RAF's airfields.

▷ **Junkers Ju-87 dive bombers**, known as Stukas. These German aircraft dived straight down on to their targets, which helped their pilots to aim the bombs accurately. A Stuka attack was made more terrifying for people on the ground by the wailing noise from a siren it carried. The Junkers Ju-88 (on the poster, left) was a bigger aircraft, with two engines. It was also used as a dive bomber.

STUKAS

JUNKERS FLUGZEUG- UND -MOTORENWERKE A.-G., DESSAU

5

GETTING READY

People in Britain expected that the Germans would bomb cities as well as airfields. Civilians and buildings had to be protected. A new service was set up, called Air Raid Precautions (ARP). By September 1939, there were more than 1.5 million ARP wardens.

△ **A poster** warning people of the dangers of getting off buses during blackouts.

ARP and other services got to work immediately. Sandbags were piled around the doors and windows of buildings to prevent damage from bomb blasts. At night, a 'blackout' was ordered, so that town lights would not guide enemy aircraft to their targets. Street lights were switched off, and car drivers were forbidden to use headlights. The wardens made sure people obeyed these rules.

One of the biggest fears was of poison gas. The government handed out 38 million gas masks. People were supposed to carry them wherever they went. In school, children practised wearing the masks. To indicate danger, the tops of pillar boxes were coated with a special paint that would change colour when poison gas was around.

△ **White lines** were painted on the pavements in Ealing, London. There were three lanes, one marked 'Shoppers Only'. The idea was to stop people bumping into each other in the blackout.

▷ **The entrance to a government building in London is surrounded with sandbags** to protect doors and windows from bomb-blast. Barrage balloons were put up to deter bombers.

There was a rush to build air raid shelters. Many towns had large public shelters. In London, people spent the nights in Underground stations. Over 1.5 million households in London were given shelters made of corrugated iron, called Anderson shelters after the Home Secretary, Sir John Anderson.

ARP wardens warned people of an air raid by sounding a siren. The wailing noise was a signal to go to the nearest shelter. When danger was past, the siren sounded again, meaning 'All Clear'. During the Phoney War, there were frequent practise warnings.

◁ **(Top) Anderson shelters are delivered to Londoners** in February 1939. The curved sheets were bolted together and covered with soil. The first air-raid warning (in the photo, left) was on 3 September 1939.

▽ **Getting the shelter ready.** During the Blitz many people spent every night in their cramped shelters.

BOMBS FALL ON LONDON

Hitler's pilots were ordered to bomb shipping, docks, railway yards, factories and airfields, but not cities. In August 1940 a load of bombs was dropped on London by mistake. The British took revenge by bombing the German capital city, Berlin.

▷ **German Dornier bombers over London** on the night of 7 September 1940. Searchlights help the aim of the anti-aircraft (AA or ack-ack) guns below.

△ **RAF cap badge.** Of the RAF's victory in the Battle of Britain, Churchill said, "Never... was so much owed by so many to so few."

Hitler was enraged, and ordered a massive attack on London. On 7 September 1940, the Germans launched their first 'terror raid'. Over 350 bombers, escorted by 650 fighter aircraft, flew across the Channel from France in broad daylight. They dropped more than 300 tonnes of bombs on the docks and streets of the East End area of the city.

Some of the bombs were high explosive. The rest were incendiary (fire) bombs, which threw out flaming pellets. Woolwich Arsenal, a gasworks and many of the docks along the River Thames were set on fire. Paint, rum and sugar from the huge warehouses blazed on the water.

▽ **RAF Spitfire fighter aircraft** fly over an airfield in Kent during the 'Battle of Britain' in September 1940. Fewer than 100 British pilots stopped the German airforce from destroying all their airfields.

△ **New Prime Minister Winston Churchill** looks at bomb damage in the City of London.

That night, more bombers returned, all carrying high explosive bombs. By the next morning, more than 450 Londoners lay dead, and another 1,600 were injured. Large parts of the East End were still blazing. The fumes from the warehouses almost stifled the firemen as they fought the flames.

For the next 11 weeks, London was bombed every night (except one, when the weather was too bad). Most bombs fell on Stepney, Lambeth, Deptford and other parts of the East End. Later, the West End was also hit. Buckingham Palace was damaged by bombs, but the king, George VI, did not leave London.

Large areas of the City were destroyed or burned down. There were not enough firemen or hoses to cope with the flames, which blazed out of control. And less than half the population of London had proper air raid shelters.

◁ **ARP wardens and residents inspect a house in London** destroyed the night before by a direct hit from a German bomb, in August 1940. Repair work has already started on the neighbouring house.

THE EVACUEES

Even before war began, the British government made plans to evacuate (move) town children to the countryside. Here, they would be far away from the danger of bombs. "Mothers, send them out of London!", said one poster. But many children were unhappy at being sent away from home.

▽ **Schoolchildren leave London in June 1940** on their way to the safety of the west country. Some of the things the children carried to their new homes included:

- gas mask (shown below)
- name label
- night clothes
- toothbrush
- family photographs (shown below)
- soap and towel
- playthings (shown below)
- teddy bear
- overcoat.

The evacuation began on 1 September 1939 – two days before war was declared. In big cities, thousands of children were taken to railway stations. The youngest were accompanied by their mothers or teachers, but most were to travel alone. Their names were written on armbands or on labels which were tied to their coats.

Within three days, nearly 1.5 million evacuees were on the move. Many had long train journeys. Some Londoners were sent as far as Cornwall or Wales. They were taken to live with local families in small towns and villages.

◁ **Londoners shelter from the bombs on the platform of an Underground station**. Thousands of parents refused to send their children away, feeling that they were safer and happier at home in spite of the bombs. Some town schools even held lessons in air raid shelters.

Households were paid for looking after the children, but only enough for food, bedding and spare clothes. Many evacuees were welcomed by their hosts, but others were treated as a nuisance. Country people were often shocked by the rudeness and dirtiness of some town children. A large number, especially those from very poor slum areas, had only ragged clothes and were infested with lice. Most knew nothing about the countryside, and were amazed by the quietness.

But mothers and children were not the only evacuees. Patients from city hospitals were sent to care homes in the country. This left the hospitals free to look after people wounded by the bombing. Animals from Chessington Zoo, near London, were taken to Devon.

LEAVE THIS TO US SONNY — YOU OUGHT TO BE OUT OF LONDON

MINISTRY OF HEALTH EVACUATION SCHEME

△ **Many evacuees quickly became bored or homesick in the country.** They missed the bustle of the streets, cinemas and chip shops. By early 1940, a million mothers and children had returned to the towns. This government poster warned children of the dangers there.

▷ **A policewoman ties a girl's evacuation label** on to her coat in October 1939.

(ARP) THE BLITZ OUTSIDE LONDON

Soon after the first raid on London, the German air force began bombing ports and factory towns in South Wales and Merseyside. But these were well defended by RAF fighters and anti-aircraft guns. In November 1940, the Germans turned to easier targets.

▷ **King George VI and Queen Elizabeth** (the present queen's parents) visited bombed areas of cities to cheer people up.

△ **A street in Coventry set alight by fire bombs** in the raid of 14 November 1940. The bombs started over 200 fires, destroyed 60,000 buildings and blocked the railway lines. Water mains were smashed, and firefighters had to collect water from the river. Telephones and electricity supplies were also put out of action. The city had only 40 anti-aircraft guns to defend it.

INCENDIARY BOMB

Pin this inside your front door

REMEMBER YOUR GAS-MASK

△ **A government poster** warns of the danger of incendiary (fire) bombs and reminds people to carry their gas masks.

The first was Coventry. On the night of 14 November, more than 400 German bombers flew over the city. They dropped fire bombs, high explosive bombs and land mines. Several factories and most of the town centre, including the ancient cathedral, were destroyed. At least 520 people were killed.

Two weeks later, Liverpool suffered its first blitz. Then it was the turn of Southampton and Bristol. By mid-December, the Germans were bombing industrial cities such as Sheffield and Birmingham. One of the worst raids of all struck Manchester just before Christmas. For 36 hours, waves of bombers droned over the city. Incendiary bombs started huge fires. Then the blast from high explosive bombs fanned the flames into a raging 'fire storm'. In early 1941, Britain's major cities suffered even more. In Portsmouth, 930 civilians were killed in a single raid and, in Hull, 1,000 killed in two raids. At Clydebank, only seven out of 12,000 homes were left undamaged.

Much of Britain was now in the front line of the war. In the first eight months of the Blitz, over 20,000 Londoners were killed. Another 23,000 died outside London. Hitler had believed that this 'terror bombing' would scare the British into surrendering. But by February 1941, he realized that his campaign was not working. The bombing, he said, had failed to break the "will to resist of the English people".

◁ **Firemen work on** as a building collapses during the Manchester firestorm.

▽ **The wreckage of York railway station** after an air raid in 1942.

THE RESCUE SERVICES

Night after night, the fire services fought to control the many fires caused by incendiary bombs. Besides the regular firemen, there were 60,000 volunteers in the Auxiliary Fire Service. Many were on duty for two days at a time with little opportunity to sleep.

The firefighters were in constant danger from heat, fumes and falling buildings, as well as the bombs dropping all around. They often ran out of water because the mains pipes were smashed by bombs. And there were not enough fire engines. Many countryside fire brigades came to help the city services, but found that their hoses would not fit the city water pipes.

Boys pull pieces from a crashed German aircraft. Many children had collections of war trophies, like those shown below. But there was always danger from unexploded bombs.

◁ **Rescue workers search for survivors in the ruins of a house.** All wear tin hats to protect them against falling rubble. 'W' stands for Warden, 'SP' for Stretcher Party and 'R' for Rescue.

▷ **Members of the voluntary services** serve food and drinks to rescue workers and people left homeless by the bombing.

▽ **A blitzed part of central London**, with the street strewn with bricks and glass.

Like the firemen, ambulance and other medical workers often went into action during the raid itself. Doctors and nurses gave first-aid to injured people, and stretcher parties carried them to the ambulances. Many of these helpers were volunteers.

But the dead and wounded often lay trapped beneath tonnes of rubble. Most streets were blocked too, with cars and buses overturned. It was the job of the Heavy Rescue Squad to clear away this wreckage. They used ropes and chains to drag away fallen beams, and propped up dangerous walls.

The air raids were mostly at night. During the day, people worked hard repairing the damage. Engineers tried to mend shattered water pipes and electricity cables. Soldiers, volunteers and rescue squads carried on clearing streets and carting away the rubble. The most dangerous job of all belonged to the Bomb Disposal Squad. They had to deal with the many bombs and mines which had landed without exploding.

The muddle and chaos made it easy for criminals to work. A growing number of muggers and pickpockets attacked people in the blackout. 'Looters' (thieves) stole goods from damaged shops and houses.

BLACK-OUT
ZERO
HOUR
TO-NIGHT
UNTIL 5.15 A.M.
MOON 5.17 MOON 2.13
RISES SETS

SMILING THROUGH

"Keep smiling through", sang Vera Lynn, in one of the most popular songs of the war. But by May 1941, over 1.4 million people had lost their homes. Many thousands had also had family or friends killed or badly injured in the Blitz or in combat overseas.

Some homeless people moved in with relatives or friends. Others had to go to the nearest rest centre – usually a church hall or school – until a new home could be found. There they were given food and somewhere to sleep. Even those who still had homes were unable to cook because there were no electricity, gas or water supplies. Hot meals and drinks were provided at emergency centres and mobile canteens in each town.

▷ **Life goes on in a bombed street.** Workmen repair the damaged road. Metal scrap is collected to be made into weapons, and the grocer has opened as usual. Foods like meat, butter, eggs, sugar and cheese were in short supply and people were only allowed a small ration, or amount, of these each week.

◁ **Nurses at a hospital clear up after an air raid.** City hospitals were packed with patients during the Blitz. The injured were soon sent home to make room for others. Extra hospitals had to be opened up in the nearby countryside.

▷ **A lesson in an air raid shelter.** Many schools had to be closed because of bomb damage or to be used as rescue centres for the injured.

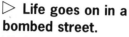

ALDEN ROAD.

CAPSTAN

BREAD

PUBLIC SHELTER

BUSINESS AS USUAL

OPEN

SPITFIRE Do it NOW

ROAD CLOSED

Hundreds of shops and offices were also ruined by the bombing, yet people were determined to carry on. Shopkeepers covered their smashed windows with plywood and put up notices boasting "Business as Usual". Damaged goods were sold off cheaply in street auctions. Without electricity, office staff got used to working by candlelight.

Buses, trams and trains still ran, though there were fewer than in peacetime. Postmen and milkmen scrambled through the rubble to make their deliveries. Clergymen held regular services in bombed-out churches. Bomb sites were also used for open-air concerts and dances. Many cinemas, music halls and theatres stayed open for shows throughout the war.

◁ **A poster showing Winston Churchill**, who had become Prime Minister in 1940. Churchill's speeches encouraged the British to keep fighting.

▽ **A dance hall in Lewisham is used as a centre** to support bombed-out Londoners (below left).

▽ **A defiant notice** outside a London cinema.

FIRE

THE BAEDEKER BOMBINGS

By June 1941, Hitler had given up his plan to invade Britain. He moved many of his aircraft to help the German attack on the Soviet Union. As a result, there were fewer raids on British towns. But soon the RAF began its own terror bombings on Germany. On 28 March 1942, British bombers raided the port of Lübeck.

THE ATTACK BEGINS IN THE FACTORY

▽ **Canterbury lies in ruins** after three nights of bombing in June 1942. Above the smoking wreckage towers the cathedral, which was only slightly damaged. Nearly 500 buildings were destroyed in the raids.

The German bombers were guided to their targets by following two beams of radio signals from fighter aircraft. The target was at the point where the beams crossed. The leading aircraft dropped flares to light up the area.

△ **A British poster shows RAF Lancaster bombers attacking a German city.** It was displayed in aircraft factories to show the workers the importance of their jobs.

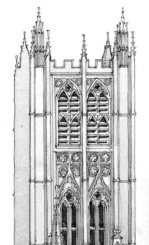

RIVERS ST MEWS

Lübeck was an ancient and beautiful town. It had little defence, and was not an important military base. The aim of the mission was to show the power of the bombers and to destroy the homes of German civilians. It was the heaviest RAF raid so far in the war, killing over 300 people. Immediately, Hitler ordered a series of revenge attacks on British cities. He chose historic places, which appeared in the German Baedeker guide book for tourists. So, on April 24, the 'Baedeker Raids' began.

The first target was Exeter. A small force of German bombers ruined the city centre, including the medieval cathedral. The next night, a larger force crossed the Channel and headed north. The defenders thought it was aiming for factories at Bristol. Instead, the Germans bombed the unprepared city of Bath. They killed 400 people and destroyed many buildings. Over 10,000 civilians fled Bath and took refuge in the fields.

▷ **A tunnel in the London Underground is turned into an electronics factory.** Here it was safe from bombs.

▽ **A captured German air crew** is marched away after being shot down. Behind them, smoke rises from their burning bomber.

◁ **A church, with all but the spire destroyed** during a Baedeker bombing raid on the West Country spa city of Bath. Many of the tall Georgian buildings were made of thin Bath stone, which collapsed easily. Hundreds of people were buried alive. Others were hit by machine gun fire from the bombers. Altogether, there were 12 Baedeker Raids on six tourist cities. More than 2,500 civilians were killed.

During the next two months, Norwich, York and Canterbury were also attacked. None of these tourist cities had enough AA guns or barrage balloons.

But soon the RAF was able to hit back. Fighter aircraft, fitted with radar (which helped detect enemy aircraft in the dark), shot down 17 German bombers. Then, on 31 May, more than 1,000 British bombers attacked the German city of Cologne. This was followed by massive raids on other industrial towns in Germany.

DOODLE-BUGS AND ROCKETS

There was a lull in bombing during early 1944, as the Allies gained control of the air and invaded occupied France. Then the Germans launched a terrifying new weapon. It was a flying bomb. Aimed from France, its engine stopped over Britain. It dived to the ground with a tonne of high explosive.

▽ **A Tempest fighter aircraft chases a V-1 flying bomb over Kent.** Some pilots brought down V-1s by flipping them over with their wing tips. But most shot them down with cannon shells.

△ **The wreckage caused in a street** in Hornsey, London, by a V-2 rocket in November 1944. Soaring to 96 kilometres high, the V-2 hurtled down again at a speed of 5,700 kph. South-east London and Kent suffered worst during the V-1 and V-2 blitzes. But Northern and Midland counties were also V-1 targets.

This was known as the V-1. It looked like a tiny aircraft, but had no pilot. During the next nine months, almost 8,000 were launched towards Britain. Over 2,000 actually hit London, and these caused massive damage. They killed over 6,000 Londoners and wrecked half a million homes. One flying bomb landed on the Guards Chapel at the Wellington Barracks during a Sunday service, killing 119 people.

The public were shocked by the sinister V-1s (also known as doodle-bugs or buzz-bombs). Thousands of evacuees had come back to London during 1944. Now they quickly left again. Over 2,500 anti-aircraft guns were moved to the south coast to try to shoot down the V-1s before they reached London.

◁ **British soldiers inspect bomb damage to V-1 launch pads** in northern France in spring 1945.

▷ **A little girl, injured in a flying bomb blast in Victoria** in London, is carried to safety by a rescue worker.

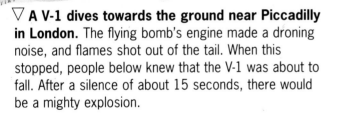

▽ **A V-1 dives towards the ground near Piccadilly in London.** The flying bomb's engine made a droning noise, and flames shot out of the tail. When this stopped, people below knew that the V-1 was about to fall. After a silence of about 15 seconds, there would be a mighty explosion.

There was worse to come. In the early evening of 8 September, the first German V-2 rocket was fired at Britain from a base on the Continent. With a huge double bang it fell on Chiswick, causing three deaths.

The V-2s produced even greater terror and damage than the doodle-bugs. More than 500 landed in the London area, killing 2,855 people. They flew so fast and high that there was no warning of their approach. Anti-aircraft guns and fighter aircraft had no chance of hitting them. RAF bombers desperately tried to find and destroy the V-2 launch bases in the Netherlands and Germany.

VICTORY AT LAST 1945

By late March 1945, the Allied armies had advanced deep into Germany. They captured the enemy airfields and rocket launching sites. The Germans were fast running out of fuel – and aircraft. There were only 12 bombers in the last raid, on eastern England.

▽ **Coventry Cathedral** immediately after the bombing in November 1940 and the ruins today (inset).

The last V-2 rocket of the war hit Orpington in Kent on 27 March 1945. One person died. Two days later, the last V-1 splashed on to a sewage farm in Hertfordshire. The Blitz was over. Hitler's attempt to bomb the British into surrender had failed. Now RAF and United States' bombers pounded German cities almost every night.

On 30 April, the German capital Berlin was overrun by the Soviet Army. In the face of defeat, Hitler killed himself, and four days later the Germans surrendered. In Britain, the government named 8 May 1945 as Victory in Europe (VE) Day.

VE day – celebrations (above) and newspaper report (right).

GLOSSARY

barrage balloon a large balloon held to the ground by a cable. Enemy aircraft could not fly low for fear of hitting the cable or balloon.

blackout turning off outside lights and hiding all artificial light within buildings so that German bombers could not locate cities and towns from the air.

bomber a slow, powerful aircraft large enough to carry a load of bombs.

civilian a person who does not belong to the armed forces.

fighter a small, fast aircraft used to attack enemy bombers.

fire storm a violent blaze in which flames cause hot air to rise quickly, creating a wind that keeps the fire going.

gas mask a mask worn over the face. It has a filter to clean the air which is breathed in.

mine a device which explodes when touched. The Germans dropped mines with parachutes.

Nazis supporters of Hitler's National Socialist Party.

rationing the sharing out of goods which are in short supply so that everyone gets an equal amount.

searchlight powerful spotlight shone into the sky to pick out enemy aircraft.

Soviet Union the union of many countries in Asia and Eastern Europe, among them Russia, Lithuania, Latvia and Georgia, now split up. Also known as the USSR (Union of Soviet Socialist Republics).

volunteer someone who offers to help.

Britain in the Blitz.
This map shows the main places which were hit by German bombs and V-2 rockets between May 1940 and March 1945.

V-1s reaching towns in the Midlands and North of England were launched from German aircraft flying over the North Sea.

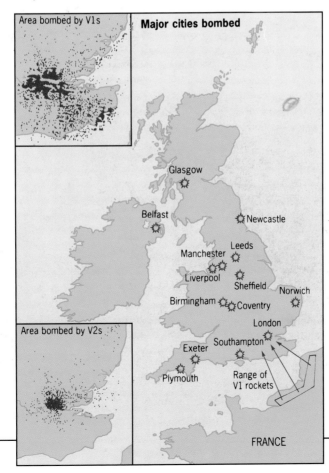

Area bombed by V1s

Major cities bombed

Area bombed by V2s

Glasgow

Belfast

Newcastle

Leeds

Manchester

Liverpool

Sheffield

Norwich

Birmingham

Coventry

London

Exeter

Southampton

Plymouth

Range of V1 rockets

FRANCE

TIMECHART

1939
September 1: First evacuation from towns.
September 3: Britain declares war on Germany.
1940
January 8: Food rationing begins.
May 3: German bomber crashes at Clacton, killing two civilians — the first mainland deaths of the war.
May 9: Winston Churchill becomes Prime Minister.
June 4: British forces retreat from France via the port of Dunkirk.
August 8: Battle of Britain between German and British air forces begins.
September 7: First German bombing raid on London.
November 14: Air raid on Coventry.
1941
January 2: German planes bomb southern Ireland despite it not being involved in the war.
June 1: Clothes are rationed.
December: United States (US) joins the war.
1942
January 26: US troops arrive in Northern Ireland.
March 28: Massive RAF raid on Lübeck.
April 24: Baedeker Raids begin with attack on Exeter.
1943
July 31: Massive RAF raid on Hamburg.
1944
June 6: D-Day invasion of France by Allied troops.
June 13: First V-1s land in Britain.
September 8: First V-2 rocket hits London.
1945
March: Last German bomber raid; last V-1 and V-2.
May 8: VE-Day celebrations, with street parties, fireworks and bonfires.

INDEX

24